Grandma's Garden
A Growing Adventure

Author: Kimberly Rosemay

Illustrator: Lidya Riani

Dream Rocket Books | Dream Journey Kids Publishing | Sheridan Wyoming

DREAM JOURNEY KIDS PUBLISHING

201 East 5th Street, Suite 1200. Sheridan, Wyoming 82801
dreamjourneykidspublishing.com

Copyright © 2020 Kimberly Rosemay. All rights reserved.

Thank you for purchasing an authorized copy of this book. For permission requests, write to the publisher, addressed "Attention: Permissions" at:
permissions@dreamjourneykidspublishing.com

Dream Rocket Books is an imprint of Dream Journey Kids Publishing

Printed in the United States of America.
First edition 2020
1 2 3 4 5 6 7 8 9 10
Library of Congress Control Number: 2020909024

Publisher's Cataloging-In-Publication Data
(Prepared by The Donohue Group, Inc.)

Names: Rosemay, Kimberly, author. | Riani, Lidya, illustrator.
Title: Grandma's garden : a growing adventure / author: Kimberly Rosemay ; illustrator: Lidya Riani.
Description: First printing edition. | Sheridan, Wyoming : Dream Rocket Books, [an imprint of] Dream Journey Kids Publishing, 2020. | Interest age level: 004-008. | Summary: "A rhyming tale of an adventurous journey seen through the eyes of this happy go lucky youngster as she explores the natural beauty in her Grandma's Garden. A little added sparkle of magnificent imagination and a whole new secret garden comes alive as little critters and friends come to play"--Provided by publisher.
Identifiers: ISBN 9781735072111 (hardcover) | ISBN 9781735072128 (paperback) | ISBN 9781735072104 (ebook)
Subjects: LCSH: Gardens--Juvenile fiction. | Grandmothers--Juvenile fiction. | Imagination--Juvenile fiction. | Garden animals--Juvenile fiction. | CYAC: Gardens--Fiction. | Grandmothers--Fiction. | Imagination--Fiction. | Garden animals--Fiction. | LCGFT: Stories in rhyme.
Classification: LCC PZ7.1.R6699 Gr 2020 (print) | LCC PZ7.1.R6699 (ebook) | DDC [E]--dc23

* This publication is also available in:

(Audio-CD) ISBN: 978-1-7350721-4-2 and (Downloadable Audio File) ISBN: 978-1-7350721-3-5

Any references to historical events, real people, or real places are used fictitiously.
Names, characters, and places are products of the author's imagination.

For my beautiful Brooklyn Journey
-Thank you for your sunshine!

In Grandma's garden, lisianthus grow...

pink and white blossoms in every row.

At this little house at the end of the road butterflies dance in the sunlight, under the alcove. A perfect place...

for the magical journey of a girl named Koko.

Soon, in blows the sweet smell of tiger lilies
as it floats in the air past bluebird's tweedle-dees.
Nesting soft as a feather, warm and cozy
with a bird's eye view high in the tree
but there was one thing Koko found more lovely

Then, one, two, three, busy bees whiz by on honey-powered scooters as they race to the hive

It's the last haul of nectar before midday arrives.
And the buzz around town: "it's the sweetest job in the skies!"
but there was one thing Koko loved more than honey!

Just around the corner, squirrels play hide and seek
Peekaboo through the bushes with acorns in their cheeks

One spies behind a tree to take a sneak peek
And is tagged on the shoulder! As he lets out a shriek.

but there was one thing Koko found more fancy-free! And meanwhile...

The caressing breeze tickles Koko's feet
and melts away any worries of the summer's heat.

And through misty air from the fountain's peak
You may see tiny somersaulting rainbows leap

but there was one thing Koko found more unique!

for a fun-filled adventure through the rows of veggies

Fresh tomatoes, sweet peppers, carrots, herbs, and snap peas
Make some of our family's yummiest recipes.

Yet there was something that made Koko even more full of glee.

Then suddenly, someone lets out a bellow...
And clamoring sounds can be heard from below.
Heaveeeee ho! Is the sound at the mound of dirt!
Pharaoh Ants in their kingdom very hard at work.

Heave-ho! Once more with a little gusto
And up to the top of the anthill they go.
Still, there was one thing Koko found much more dynamo!

Up above, summer skies seem forever,
but don't blink your eyes.

You may miss the bubble-breathing dragonflies.

In Grandma's garden, swooping arms lift me high to catch floating bubbles as they pop, pop, pop, in the sky.

But there was one thing that made Koko more satisfied!

Later, dreamy lullabies Mommy sings for me,

Aunty Brianna preps lemonade for everybody,

and a bottle for me.

"Just like the plants in Grandma's garden, I grow steadily

Every step you take, I follow your lead

And maybe one day I'll be as tall as a tree
But for now, I am happily wild and carefree
At last, there's one thing I love, most definitely!"

"And that's my super-fantastic, wonderful Granny!"
And all of a sudden, there it was...

Grandma's swirling, magical, amazing, epic hug.

Sweet, fancy-free, lovely, caressing, yippee!

Warm, light and fuzzy most definitely!
The best ever feeling!

...Well, next to Mommy's!

And later, friends arrive... Sally's brought apple pie.

And Faye whispers, "Look at how much the baby's grown, oh my!"

In Grandma's garden, come meet us all there
Where there's friendship, fun, and laughter.
Let's all have some cheer.

While the sunset fades blue to pink hues of light
Fireflies flicker in the glow of twilight

Joyful chatter fills the air 'til the very last goodbye
And it's quiet once again on this warm summer's night

Now, at this very moment, it's just Grandma and me
And there's no place more magical than in her company.

For in Grandma's garden, Grandma holds me tightly.
As she kisses me gently. I D- R- I- F- T,

Fast asleep.

- Thank Goodness for Grandas! -